ANATOMY

Overhead Transparencies • Student Reproducibles • Assessment Tools

Contributing Writers
Joellyn Cicciarelli
Alaska Hults

Editor: Alaska Hults
Illustrators: Diane Valko, Marion Eldridge
Cover and Transparency Illustrator: David Christensen
Designer: Mary Gagné
Cover Designer: Mary Gagné
Art Director: Tom Cochrane
Project Director: Carolea Williams

Table of Contents

Introduction

Welcome to the fascinating world of the human body! With over 200 bones, 600 muscles, and 100,000 heartbeats a day, we are arguably one of the most efficient "machines" in existence.

Anatomy explains to students the mystery of the human body in meaningful, interesting ways. Basic facts are interwoven with hands-on activities, including at least one activity in each section that encourages students to be involved in their community. Five full-color transparencies help students visualize the functions of each system of the human body. Students practice the following skills while exploring the body's system: listening and speaking, researching, reading and writing, and problem solving.

Each of the five sections in this resource features information and activities related to a different system of the human body. Before students begin each section, draw a KWL chart. Label the three columns *What We **K**now, What We **W**ant to Know,* and *What We **L**earned.* Have students discuss what they already know about that system of the body, and record their responses in the first column. Then, have students discuss what questions they still have, and record them in the second column. Display the transparency for the section, and have students read and discuss the information on it.

Have students complete the activities in each section individually, in pairs, in small groups, or together as a whole class. If you choose to have students work individually or at a center, provide books that will help them find additional information on each topic. After students have completed the reading and activities for a section, ask them what they learned about the topic. Record their responses in the third column of the KWL chart. Then, assign the What Did You Learn? page in each section as a cumulative quiz to assess student learning. Students will find the answers in the activities they completed and in the transparency for the section.

Skull
Mandible
Clavicle
Scapula
Sternum
Ribs
Humerus
Vertebral Column
Vertebrae
Ulna
Ilium
Radius
Carpals
Metacarpals
Femur
Patella
Tibia
Fibula
Metatarsals
Tarsals

The Brain

The brain is a soft, jelly-like mass inside the skull that controls thinking, voluntary and involuntary movement, speech, and the five senses.

The brain is made up of neurons, cells that are specialized to receive and send messages throughout parts of the body. Messages are received from the senses and interpreted by the brain. The brain then sends back orders to the muscles and glands in response to the interpreted message.

There are three main parts of the brain: the cerebrum, the cerebellum, and the brain stem. The cerebrum, the upper part of the brain, is responsible for higher mental activities. The cerebellum, located in the back of the cerebrum, controls the body's sense of position. The brain stem controls involuntary body processes.

THE BRAIN

The three main parts of the brain control different body functions. Label the diagram below, writing the bold words in the correct part of the brain.

The Cerebrum Controls	The Cerebellum Controls	The Brain Stem Controls
thinking **memory** **planning** **body movement** **touch interpretation** **hearing** **smell** **vision** **speech** **taste**	**balance** **coordination** **posture**	**breathing** **heartbeat** **digestion** **sleepiness** **wakefulness**

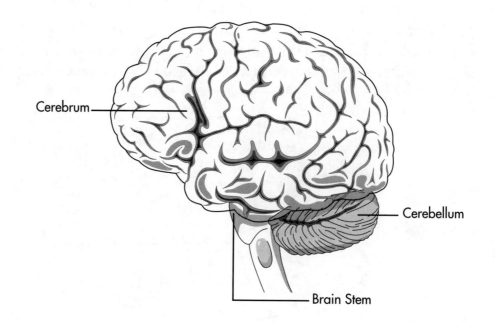

Cerebrum

Cerebellum

Brain Stem

Testing Reflexes

The nervous system is the body's control and communication center. The nervous system consists of the brain, spinal cord, and nerves. These body parts work together to control many important physical functions such as how a person moves, thinks, and feels pain or pleasure.

Nerves receive sensory messages from the body and send them up the spinal cord to the brain. The brain interprets the messages and sends responses through the spinal cord to the nerves throughout the body. The brain's response causes the body to react. For example, if a person touches a flame, nerves in the finger send a message to the brain that the person is touching something hot. The brain sends a response back, causing the muscles in the person's arm and hand to move away from the stove. The person then feels pain.

Sometimes the nervous system works so quickly that a person may not even be aware that the brain, spinal cord, and nerves are at work. When quick responses are required, the nerve connection to the brain can be bypassed. To save time, the spinal cord takes over the brain's job and instructs the body to move. These quick-moving messages and responses along the nervous system are called reflex actions or reflexes.

REFLEX TESTS

You can demonstrate the quick responses of the nervous system by performing the following reflex tests. After each test, tell what you think the original nerve message was, how the body showed a reflex action, and how long you estimate it took for the body to react.

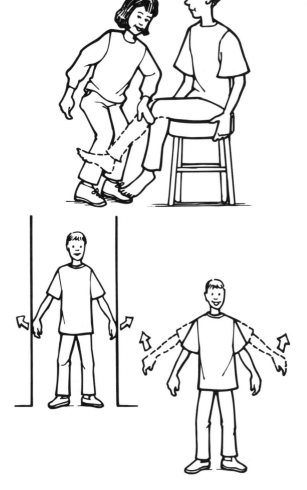

1. Clap your hands about two feet in front of a partner's eyes. His or her eyes should blink.

2. Have a partner sit on a stool and dangle his or her legs. Use your hand to tap just below your partner's knee. Your partner's leg will kick outward.

3. With the light on, look at the size of a partner's pupils. Turn off the light. Notice how the pupils get bigger.

4. Have a partner stand in a doorway. Have your partner press his or her hands against the sides of the doorway, as hard as possible, for 30 seconds. Have your partner step away from the doorway and relax his or her arms. The arms should begin to rise.

Nerve Task Cards

NOTE TO TEACHER:
There are dozens of ways to use these task cards. Here are just a few…

- Laminate cards, cut them out, and place them in a learning center.
- Send a task card with each student during library research time.
- Assign cards as a long-term homework project or as extra credit.
- Pass cards out randomly, one to each student. Have students form groups according to card tasks to complete the tasks together.

Sensory nerves are like mail carriers. They carry messages about the five senses, pain, and pleasure from your body, through the spinal cord, and to your brain.

Design a sensory nerve mailbag. Cover your bag with information about your job as a sensory nerve. Fill the mailbag with postcard messages addressed from body parts to the brain.

Nerves function because chemical reactions inside the neurons send electricity through your body.

Research to find out why people are struck by lightning. Draw an illustration to show what occurs. Under your drawing, write a paragraph that explains the connection between lightning and the electricity in your body.

A nerve is a bundle of cells called neurons that are arranged like the wires in a telephone cable. These "wires" are used to relay messages between your brain and your body.

Imagine that you are a "telephone" operator inside a nerve. Choose a body action and tape-record a three-way telephone conversation between the nerve, the brain, and the body part you want to move.

Neurons are not connected. For a message to travel from one neuron to another, a chemical called a neurotransmitter is released into a synapse, the gap between two neurons. The neurotransmitter allows the message to move from one neuron to another.

Dreams are evidence that the neurons in your brain are working even when you sleep. Keep a pencil and paper next to your bed for a week. When you wake up each morning, write down a dream you remember. Share your dreams with classmates.

The funny bone is not a bone. It is a nerve that is less protected than other nerves. When you hit that part of the elbow, the sensation you feel is a nerve impulse traveling down your arm.

Think about a time when you hit your funny bone. Write a paragraph that uses at least five adjectives, one simile, and one metaphor to describe the sensation you felt.

Before birth, the body makes 250,000 neurons a minute. After birth, no more neurons are made. Neurons may be destroyed through injury, disease, aging, drug use, or alcohol use.

Research brain damage. Design a poster that promotes brain damage prevention.

Connector nerves are in the spinal cord and brain. These nerves process information that is being sent between the body, brain, and spinal cord.

Imagine your connector nerves were processing everything backward for one day. For example, if you touched a hot stove you would feel ice cold. Write a story about your experiences.

Motor nerves send messages from the brain and spinal cord to initiate motion in the muscles and glands.

Choose five muscles and five internal organs. Imagine that a message is being sent from the brain to each muscle and organ through a motor nerve. Write a sentence for each body part explaining what the brain is commanding it to do.

Community Action Project

The Spinal Cord

The spinal cord is a long string of nerve tissue leading down the back. The spinal cord acts as a two-way tunnel carrying nerve impulses between the brain and nerves throughout the body.

- The spinal cord is approximately 16 inches long.
- The interior section of the spinal cord is a collection of neurons called gray matter. The gray matter is surrounded by white matter, nerves that connect the brain and the spinal cord.
- The spinal cord helps control simple reflex actions by quickly sending messages to the muscles for movement.
- The spinal cord is protected by the backbone and its vertebrae.

INFORMATION

The spinal cord is vital to body movement and function. An injury to the spinal cord can cause partial or full paralysis and sometimes death. An injury to the spinal cord usually occurs when its protection, the vertebrae in the backbone, is fractured. Accidents causing injury to the vertebrae and spinal cord are usually preventable. These injuries often occur during recreational activities such as swimming or surfing. Certain sports such as wrestling and football have also proven dangerous for the spinal cord.

Helping Others—Spinal Cord Injury Prevention Video

Research

Contact a local hospital to obtain information about spinal cord injuries, their consequences, and their prevention strategies. Use your research to make a video to teach people how to protect themselves from spinal cord injuries.

Action Plan

Use these questions to help make your plan.

- What adult can help you plan and tape the video? Which friends can help you?

- Who is your target audience? Children? Adults? Swimmers? Football players? Always keep your audience in mind.

- When and where will you present your video?

- What are two or three important ideas that you want to get across to your audience?

- What is the best way to visually give information? Will you include demonstrations of correct ways to participate in recreational activities? Interviews with doctors? Tours of potentially dangerous places where spinal cord injuries occur?

- What audio components can be added to your video? Music? Different voices for different sections? A narrator?

- How will you begin your video? With a narrated introduction? With a written introduction?

Focus on Memory

Our brains have three different types of memory—sensory memory, short-term memory, and long-term memory. We depend on a combination of all three types of memory to learn things. You can teach yourself ways to improve all three, and all three can be affected by brain damage.

• Sensory Memory

Sensory memory acts as a kind of gatekeeper to our brain, holding new information long enough to decide whether to move it to short-term memory and act on it or discard it as extra information. For example, sensory memory holds the sound you hear long enough for you to decide if you are hearing speech or music. Sensory memory lasts for only 2 to 3 seconds and we are not aware of it.

• Short-Term Memory

Short-term memory is sometimes called the working memory. We store everything we do in our short-term memory, but this information stays in our memory only for a short period. The actual amount of time we store information in short-term memory depends on a variety of factors, including how often we use the information.

• Long-Term Memory

We use long-term memory to recall information—both important and unimportant—for very long periods. This information can be for a skill, such as riding a skateboard, or for facts, such as your mother's birthday or what your soccer coach looks like. The more you use a piece of information in short-term memory, the more likely it is to become a long-term memory.

Short-Term Recall

Materials
• long, shallow container
• common, but unrelated objects (e.g., a hammer, a knitting needle, a pencil sharpener)
• large piece of cloth to cover the container
• timer

Find a partner to help you explore this activity on short-term memory. Fill a long, shallow container, such as a sweater box, with a variety of objects. Make sure the objects are not all related. For example, make sure that they are not all objects found in your classroom. Place them randomly in the container, and cover it with a piece of cloth. Set a timer for 1 minute, and remove the cloth. Challenge your partner to remember all the objects. When the timer rings, cover the objects again. Have your partner write all the objects that he or she can remember. Check your partner's list against the original box. If you have extra time, repeat the activity with new objects, but this time, arrange the objects in ways that relate them to each other, such as size, shape, or color. Can your partner remember more of the objects when they are in a pattern?

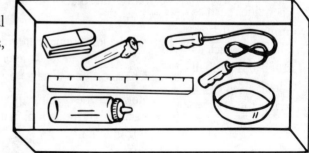

Did You Know?

Most people cannot store more than ten numbers in a series in their long-term memory. That is why combination locks, phone numbers, and other common numbers are ten digits or less.

Anatomy © 2003 Creative Teaching Press

What Did You Learn?

A. Circle the best answer.

1. The cerebellum is a

a. pathway that carries messages to the brain.
b. part of the brain that controls coordination.
c. type of nerve.
d. cell body.

2. You might use short-term memory to recall

a. your kindergarten teacher's face.
b. how to ride a bike.
c. the phone number you just looked up.
d. your brother's birthday.

3. The nervous system is made up of

a. the brain, spinal cord, and nerves.
b. nerves, blood, and brain.
c. your lungs, brain, and spinal cord.
d. your brother's birthday.

4. The best way to prevent damage to your spinal cord is to prevent damage to your

a. sofa.
b. eyes.
c. fingers.
d. backbone.

B. Draw a line from the type of memory to what it helps you remember.

Type of Memory	Helps You Remember
1. sensory memory	a. a phone number you just looked up
2. short-term memory	b. your dog's name
3. long-term memory	c. the difference between the sound of a voice and the sound of a fan

C. Fill in each blank. Use *cerebrum, cerebellum,* or *brain stem*.

1. The _____ controls balance.
2. The _____ controls breathing.

D. Explain how the spinal cord carries messages to and from the brain.

_____

_____

_____

_____

Name _____

The Heart

The heart is a strong, pear-shaped muscle. It is located between the two lungs, under the breastbone, and inside the rib cage.

The heart has two sides, and each side has two chambers. The chambers are called the atria and ventricles. The right atrium and ventricle pump blood into the lungs to pick up oxygen. The left atrium and ventricle pump the blood with oxygen back into the body.

Valves control the flow of blood through the four chambers. The valves work like trapdoors that open and close so blood cannot go back into a chamber once it is pumped out.

BLOOD FLOW

Trace the flow of blood through the heart. Use blue to trace the path of blood through the heart from the body parts to the lungs. Use red to trace the path of blood from the lungs to the body.

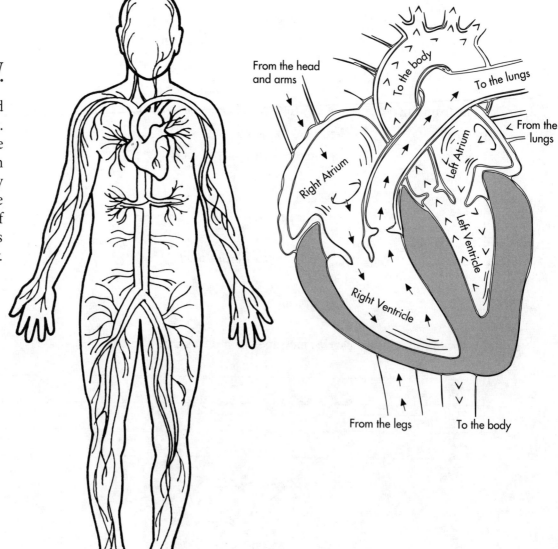

From the head and arms

To the body

To the lungs

From the lungs

Right Atrium

Left Atrium

Left Ventricle

Right Ventricle

From the legs

To the body

Testing Heart Rate During Exercise

TESTING HEART RATE

Perform this test to demonstrate the increase in heart rate during exercise.

One heartbeat is a complete contraction of the heart. The heart rate is a simple count of heart contractions. During exercise, heart rate increases because the heart must work harder to give the body the oxygen it needs.

1. Measure your heart rate by placing two fingertips on the underside of the wrist of your other hand, just below the base of the thumb.
2. Count the pulsations for thirty seconds. Multiply that number by two. That number is your resting heart rate.
3. Mark your resting heart rate on the graph below where it states *resting*.
4. Perform each of the exercises listed for one minute.
5. Immediately after each exercise, count your heart rate for thirty seconds, multiply by two, and mark the number on the graph. What do you predict will happen?

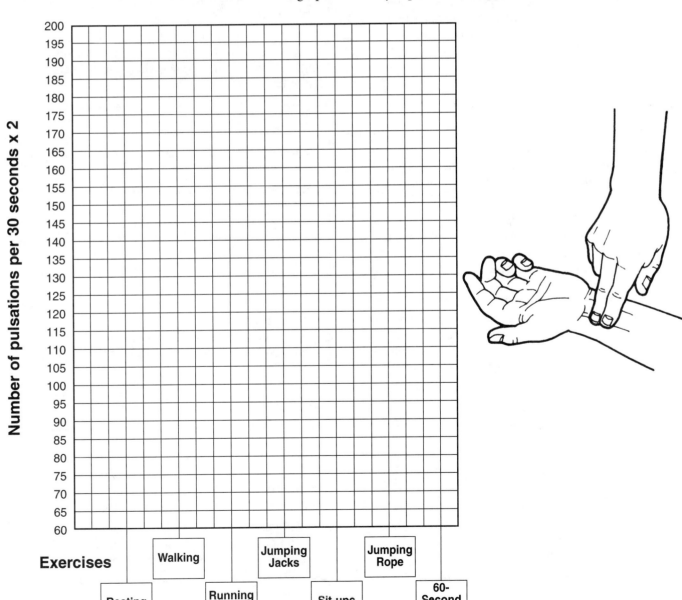

Number of pulsations per 30 seconds x 2

200
195
190
185
180
175
170
165
160
155
150
145
140
135
130
125
120
115
110
105
100
95
90
85
80
75
70
65
60

Exercises

Resting | Walking | Running in Place | Jumping Jacks | Sit-ups | Jumping Rope | 60-Second Sprint

Blood Vessel Task Cards

NOTE TO TEACHER: There are dozens of ways to use these task cards. Here are just a few…

- Laminate cards, cut them out, and place them in a learning center.
- Send a task card with each student during library research time.
- Assign cards as a long-term homework project or as extra credit.
- Pass cards out randomly, one to each student. Have students form groups according to card tasks to complete the tasks together.

Veins return blood to your heart. Very tiny veins called venules supply your veins with blood from all parts of your body.

Imagine you are a tired, deoxygenated red blood cell traveling through your veins. Write a journal entry describing your travels. Research and use the words *vein, venules, intima, venous blood, superior vena cava,* and *inferior vena cava.*

Healthy blood vessels have smooth, flexible walls. As you get older, the walls tend to harden and the inner surface of your blood vessels tends to get rough and clog from deposits of cholesterol and calcium.

Collect data about maintaining a healthy heart and blood vessels. Write and perform a public service announcement to convince people to take care of their blood vessels.

A stroke can occur when an artery to the brain clogs or ruptures. A stroke can cause a partial or total loss of consciousness, sensation, or voluntary motion.

Design an invention to help stroke victims regain control of their muscles. Draw and label your invention, and write a description.

A healthy diet helps maintain strong, unclogged blood vessels.

List everything you ate for breakfast, lunch, dinner, and snacks during the last 24 hours. Read the food pyramid. Circle all the foods that would help maintain healthy blood vessels. Underline the foods that were not good for your body.

Capillaries connect your veins and arteries at the place where the blood begins its return trip to your heart. Capillaries are barely wide enough for red blood cells to flow through them.

Make a Venn diagram to compare facts about capillaries and arteries.

Arteries carry blood away from your heart. The system of arteries is like an upside-down tree trunk with many branches that get smaller and smaller.

Draw a human body diagram. Label the heart and arteries.

Capillaries supply your body's cells with fresh oxygen and nutrients and pick up the carbon dioxide and other wastes from cells.

Imagine you are a capillary at work. Research and write a job description telling the reader what you do and why your job is important.

If your artery is cut, blood pumps out in a series of spurts timed with the heartbeat. If your vein is cut, blood flows out in an even stream.

Study first aid to learn methods to stop bleeding if a person has been cut. Design a pamphlet that explains and illustrates at least three methods.

Community Action Project

Blood

Blood is the fluid that carries nutrients, oxygen, hormones, and antibodies to the rest of the body. Blood is made of plasma, red blood cells, white blood cells, and platelets.

- Plasma is the straw-colored fluid part of the blood. The red blood cells, white blood cells, and platelets float in the plasma. Waste products from the cells and nutrients are dissolved in the plasma. Plasma is 90% water and supplies the water needed by the body's cells.
- Red blood cells give the body oxygen and nutrients. They are bright red when they carry oxygen from the lungs to the body tissues. They become bluish as they absorb carbon dioxide from body tissue and take it to the lungs. There are about 500 times more red blood cells than white blood cells.
- White blood cells are four times bigger than red blood cells. They make antibodies that attack harmful bacteria, viruses, and other foreign cells that enter the blood.
- Platelets are tiny cells that seal tears, cuts, and damaged blood vessels. They make sticky threads that form a web called a blood clot which prevents further bleeding.

INFORMATION

Sometimes a person who is ill or injured needs blood that is donated from another person. The American Red Cross organizes blood drives in order to collect blood from volunteer donors. The blood is stored in blood banks. Blood can be kept for approximately 42 days. Because blood cannot be used after that time, hospitals and health care facilities are always in need of new blood.

Helping Others—Blood Drive Campaign

Research

Contact the local chapter of the Red Cross to obtain information about the next blood drive in your area. Use this information to organize a campaign that recruits adults to participate in the next blood drive. Challenge your classmates to meet or excede the number of adults you recruit.

Action Plan

Use these questions to help make your plan.

- Sometimes it is best to avoid speaking with adults you do not know. How can you contact adults for the blood drive without having to go door to door?
- It is often difficult to convince people to give blood. What can you do or say to convince people to volunteer?
- Some people are not able to give blood due to physical conditions. What qualifications are necessary to discuss with a person who is thinking of volunteering for a blood drive?
- How will you know if a recruit actually went to the blood drive? What information do you need to have on a sign-up sheet to help gather this information?
- As you sign up recruits, what should you give them as a reminder? What other information should be given?

Focus on Blood Types

We all have a certain blood type. Scientists have given each blood type a letter. You inherit your blood type from your mother and father. You might have A, B, AB, or O blood.

• Why Does It Matter

Years ago, when doctors first tried using blood from one person in another person during a medical emergency, they found that sometimes the patient survived, and sometimes, mysteriously, the patient did not. Around 1900, a pathologist, Karl Landsteiner, figured out that there are two blood types that naturally fight each other.

• Types A, B, and AB

It was found that there are different proteins on the surface of blood cells. People with the A protein will get sick and die if they are exposed to the B protein, and people with the B protein will have the same reaction to the A protein. Each type of blood has antibodies for the other. However, if an A person marries a B person, their child will have type AB blood. A person with type AB blood can accept blood from anyone else without harm.

• Type O

There is one more group that has antibodies for both type A and B blood. People with type O blood can only accept blood from other people with O. However, they can give blood to any A, B, or AB person because there are no antibodies for the type O blood. Many people in the United States have type O blood, but it is in very high demand in blood banks. It is sometimes called the Universal Donor.

• Which Type Are You?

You can identify your blood type with a simple test at your doctor's office, but you can also get clues about your blood type if you know your parents' blood type. You can only be an O if both of your parents have type O blood. If one parent has type O and the other is parent has type A or B, you will probably have type A or B.

Chart It!

Talk to the adults in your family. Make a chart that shows all the known blood types of your relatives. Try to identify all of your relatives who share your blood type. If you are adopted, interview your classmates to find other people who share your blood type. If you do not know your blood type, have your parent call your doctor. The information is probably in your medical records. Then, present your chart of friends or relatives who share your blood type to the class.

Did You Know?

Regardless of the type of blood you have, there is always a need for donated blood. When you are old enough, you can donate a small amount of blood at a blood bank twice a year. Your body will replace the lost blood within 24 hours, and the blood you gave away may save someone's life.

What Did You Learn?

A. Circle the best answer.

1. The left side of the heart

   a. pumps deoxygenated blood.
   b. pumps blood with oxygen into the body.
   c. helps fight disease.
   d. controls balance.

2. Which statement is false?

   a. The circulatory system brings food and oxygen to all parts of the body.
   b. White blood cells help fight disease.
   c. The spinal cord is part of the circulatory system.
   d. The heart is a fist-sized, hollow muscle.

B. Draw a line to complete each sentence.

1. A healthy diet
2. Capillaries supply your blood
3. The heart is

a. with fresh oxygen and nutrients.
b. helps maintain strong, unclogged blood vessels.
c. a strong, pear-shaped muscle.

C. Fill in each blank. Use *red blood cells, white blood cells, plasma,* and *platelets.*

1. _____ can pass through a capillary wall.
2. _____ are tiny cells that seal damaged blood vessels.
3. _____ is a straw-colored fluid that carries blood cells and platelets.
4. _____ carry oxygen to different parts of the body.

D. Compare and contrast *veins* and *arteries.*

_____

_____

_____

_____

The Skeletal System

Skeleton and Bones

The skeleton provides a framework for the body. It is a mixture of bone and cartilage. The skeleton helps protect the body's vital organs. For example, the rib cage protects the heart and lungs, the skull protects the brain, and the vertebrae protect the spinal cord.

An average skeleton is made up of about 206 bones. Bones have four basic shapes: flat bone such as ribs and shoulder blades; irregular bones such as vertebrae; short bones such as those in the wrist and ankle; and long bones such as those in the arms, legs, and fingers.

Joints

The place where bones connect is called a joint. Most joints are movable. There are four basic types of movable joints. Ball-and-socket joints, such as hips and shoulders, allow bones to move in all directions. Hinge joints, such as knees and elbows, allow bones to move in only two directions. Pivot or rotating joints, such as the neck, enable bones to rotate from side to side. Gliding joints, such as those in the hands and spine, allow the flat surfaces of bones to glide over each other.

BONES

On the skeleton to the right, shade one flat bone red, one irregular bone blue, one short bone green, and one long bone yellow.

JOINTS

On the skeleton to the right, draw a box around four ball-and-socket joints, put an x on two gliding joints, circle four hinge joints, and put a star on one pivot joint.

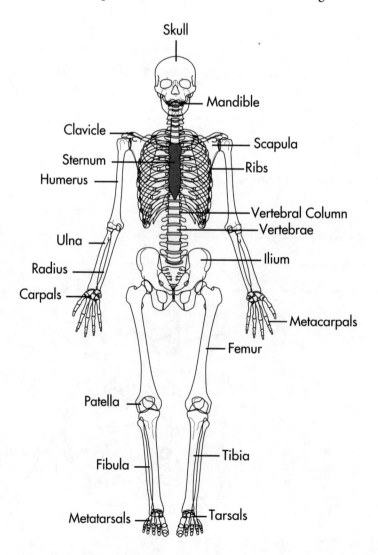

Testing Muscle Contractions

The muscular system holds the skeleton together and gives the body its build and general shape. Muscles help control body processes such as breathing, digestion, and blood flow. The muscular system consists of over 600 muscles made of long, thin fibers. Muscles work with the skeletal and nervous systems to help move the body.

Muscles work in pairs. During movement, one muscle contracts or tightens to get shorter. At the same time, the other muscle relaxes. When a movement changes direction, the muscles change actions. For example, when you bend your arm up, the bicep contracts and the tricep relaxes. But when you straighten your arm, the tricep contracts and the bicep relaxes.

MODEL ARM

Demonstrate how muscles work in pairs by following the directions to the right to build a model arm.

1. Gather three paper towel tubes, two brads, yarn or string, one permanent marker, two long balloons, masking tape, and an old glove.

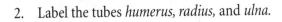

2. Label the tubes *humerus, radius,* and *ulna.*

3. Make two holes through one end of the humerus. Make two holes in the side of the radius and two holes in the side of the ulna. Attach with brads, as shown.

4. Make "muscles" by slightly inflating two long balloons. Tie knots at both ends of the balloons. Label the balloons *bicep* and *tricep.*

5. Tie the bicep muscle balloon to the humerus, radius, and ulna, as shown. Tie the tricep muscle balloon to both ends of the humerus. Tape over the tied areas.

6. Tie an old glove on the end of the radius and ulna.

7. Open and close the arm to observe muscle contractions and relaxations. Explain how this muscle works like your arm.

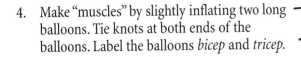
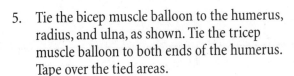

Bone and Muscle Task Cards

NOTE TO TEACHER:
There are dozens of ways to use these task cards. Here are just a few…

- Laminate cards, cut them out, and place them in a learning center.
- Send a task card with each student during library research time.
- Assign cards as a long-term homework project or as extra credit.
- Pass cards out randomly, one to each student. Have students form groups according to card tasks to complete the tasks together.

Cardiac muscles are involuntary muscles that make up the walls of your heart. The contractions of these muscles are controlled by your pacemaker, a group of specialized cells in the heart. The medulla, a part of your brain stem, controls the pacemaker.

Research CPR techniques to design a poster that shows how to restart heart muscle contractions during cardiac arrest.

Skeletal muscles are voluntary muscles that help hold the bones of your skeleton together and give your body shape. It is important to maintain strong muscles to support your body.

One way to maintain muscle strength is through exercise. Design a balanced week-long exercise program for yourself that includes at least one activity a day. Write an explanation of why you chose each exercise.

The skeleton is your body's framework. Without a skeleton, you would look like a puddle of multi-colored jelly.

Imagine that humans did not have skeletons. Make a list stating things humans could never do without a skeleton. Make another list stating things that would be easier for you to do if you had a flexible form.

Tendons are tough cords of connective collagen that allow muscles to move bones. The Achilles tendon, the largest tendon, is located just above the heel of your foot.

Research the story of Achilles in Greek mythology. Explain why the tendon above the heel is called the Achilles tendon.

Cartilage covers the ends of bones and is composed of strong protein collagen fibers. Collagen from animals is used to make gelatin.

Make a judgment as to whether humans should use animal parts such as bones to make products. Write a persuasive essay explaining your position.

Muscles contain vessels that carry blood. The blood supplies nutritional elements and oxygen to your muscle cells.

Make a chart to show ten essential nutritional elements for healthy muscles. List foods that naturally provide each element.

A broken bone is called a fracture. Most broken bones heal themselves. The healing process takes between four weeks to one year, depending on the size of the bone.

Conduct a bone fracture survey of 25 people. Collect data to document what bones were broken, how the fractures occurred, and the amount of healing time. Make a graph to show your data.

Smooth muscles are involuntary muscles controlled by your central nervous system. These muscles line the walls of most of the hollow organs in your body.

Imagine you are the central nervous system—mission control for the spaceship *S.S. Human Body*. Write a log entry that gives detailed commands to three crew members who are smooth muscles.

Anatomy © 2003 Creative Teaching Press

Community Action Project

Muscles

Muscles have three important functions. They work with the bones and the nervous system to help move the body. They help to control body processes such as breathing, digestion, and blood flow. Muscles hold the skeleton together to give the body its build and general shape.

- Muscles are strong tissue made of long thin cells called muscle fibers.
- There are more than 600 muscles in the body that are arranged in layers over the skeleton. Muscles are attached to the bones of the skeleton or to other muscles by tendons.
- Muscles are either voluntary or involuntary. Voluntary muscles, together with the bones and tendons, control all forms of conscious movement as well as automatic reactions called reflexes. Involuntary muscles are responsible for the movement of internal organs in body processes such as breathing, digestion, and heart rate.

INFORMATION

Not everyone is born with muscles that will remain healthy throughout life. Sometimes a person will develop a form of muscular dystrophy, a genetic defect that affects muscles. There are many diseases referred to as muscular dystrophy. Each form weakens skeletal muscles and seriously affects movement and posture. In some cases, muscular dystrophy forces people to use a wheelchair or shortens their life span. To date, doctors have not been able to find a cure for these diseases.

Helping Others—Muscular Dystrophy Fund-Raiser

Research

The Muscular Dystrophy Association collects money each year for research to find a cure for all types of muscular dystrophy. The money is collected on Labor Day during a nationwide telethon. Contact a local chapter of the MDA to obtain information about organizing a fund-raiser and donating money for this year's telethon.

Action Plan

Use these questions to help make your plan.

- What adult could sponsor and chaperone your fund-raiser?
- What will be the date, time, and place for the fund-raiser?
- Fund-raising activities must be easy, enjoyable, or entertaining in order for people to donate money. What could you do, sell, make, or offer to convince people to give?
- What creative ways can you think of to advertise and invite as many people as possible?
- How will you keep a record of the funds collected? Will you collect money before, during, or after the event? Will you open a bank account to hold the money until it is given to the MDA? What adult can assist you in dealing with money?
- What can you give people as a receipt for their tax-deductible donation?

Anatomy © 2003 Creative Teaching Press

What Did You Learn?

A. Circle the best answer.

1. Which statement is true?

a. The skeletal system stores calcium needed by the body.
b. The skeleton is made up entirely of cartilage.
c. Bone marrow manufactures mucus.
d. There is no such thing as a hinge joint.

2. How many muscles are there in the average person's body?

a. 80
b. over 600
c. 224
d. 2,980

3. Which system works with the skeletal and nervous systems to help move the body?

a. digestive system
b. respiratory system
c. muscular system
d. computer system

4. Which of the following is not a type of joint?

a. ball-and-socket
b. hinge
c. pivot
d. anchor

B. Draw a line from the type of joint to where it is located.

Type of Joint	Where
1. hinge joint	a. hip
2. ball-and-socket	b. neck
3. pivot	c. elbow

C. Fill in each blank.

1. Muscles hold the _____ together, help control body processes, and help move the body.
2. Muscles are attached to the bones by _____.

D. Name five bones. Tell what two of them do.

_____

_____

_____

_____

Anatomy © 2003 Creative Teaching Press

The Respiratory System

The respiratory system enables a person to breathe. Breathing consists of two basic actions: inhaling and exhaling. Inhaling is taking air into the lungs. Exhaling is pushing air out of the lungs.

When a person inhales, the diaphragm, a large dome-shaped sheet of muscle, contracts. These contractions allow the chest cavity to expand and fill the lungs with air. When a person exhales, the diaphragm relaxes. The chest cavity then contracts and pushes carbon dioxide out of the lungs. The average person inhales and exhales 15 times a minute, approximately 20,000 times a day.

INHALATION AND EXHALATION

Draw a line from each label to the appropriate section of each diagram. Some labels may be used in both diagrams.

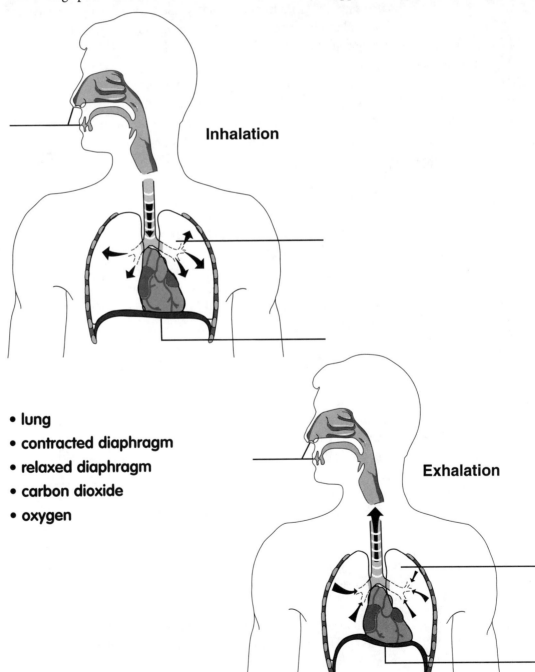

Inhalation

Exhalation

- lung
- contracted diaphragm
- relaxed diaphragm
- carbon dioxide
- oxygen

Name _____

Testing Your Lung Capacity

The main function of the respiratory system is to provide the body with the oxygen it needs to have energy and grow.

During exercise the body needs additional energy. Therefore, the body's cells need to receive more oxygen to energize the body. One way the lungs can provide extra oxygen is by increasing lung capacity, the amount of air taken into the lungs.

Lung capacity varies from person to person. Overall lung capacity for an average person is about 3,000 gallons of air per day. In other words, the average person inhales 75 million gallons of air during a lifetime.

SPIROMETER

Test your lung capacity by building and using a spirometer.

1. Gather a gallon milk jug, a piece of masking tape, a marker, a measuring cup, a small piece of cardboard, a two-foot piece of plastic tubing, a tub with water, scissors, and a cut-away top of a two-liter plastic bottle.

2. Label the milk jug in milliliters. To label, pour 60 milliliters (¹/₄ cup) into the jug. Mark it on the tape. Continue pouring and marking until you reach the top of the jug.

3. Cut tubing slits in the bottom of the cut-away top of the two-liter bottle. Push the plastic tubing through the slits.

4. To set up, fill the jug with water, hold the piece of cardboard over the mouth of the jug, and turn it over. Submerge the upside-down jug into the tub. Remove the cardboard after the jug is in the water. The jug should stay full. Arrange the jug, bottle, and tubing as shown.

5. To test, exhale a normal breath into the tubing. Water should leave the jug and enter the tub. Measure how many milliliters of water you pushed out of the jug as you exhaled. That number is your approximate normal lung capacity.

6. Refill the jug. This time exhale a large breath into the tubing. The number of milliliters pushed out is your approximate full-lung capacity.

Anatomy © 2003 Creative Teaching Press

Lung Task Cards

NOTE TO TEACHER: There are dozens of ways to use these task cards. Here are just a few…

- Laminate cards, cut them out, and place them in a learning center.
- Send a task card with each student during library research time.
- Assign cards as a long-term homework project or as extra credit.
- Pass cards out randomly, one to each student. Have students form groups according to card tasks to complete the tasks together.

If the walls of the air sacs in your lungs were spread out side by side, they would cover about half of a tennis court, approximately 1,404 square feet.

Draw and label an illustration that compares the area of the lungs' air sacs to that of a tennis court.

One function of your lungs is to help clean the blood by removing harmful substances such as fat and blood clots.

Research at least three lung functions. Imagine you were interviewing a lung. Write ten detailed questions and answers.

Humans and plants are interdependent. Humans inhale oxygen that is produced by plants and exhale carbon dioxide. In turn, plants take in that carbon dioxide and expel oxygen.

Research the oxygen cycle. Design a *Save the Rainforests* poster that uses your research as an argument for keeping the rainforests intact.

Pneumonia is a lung disease that causes the lungs' air sacs to fill with fluid and white blood cells. Pneumonia can be cured and prevented but is still a leading cause of death in the United States.

Research pneumonia. Perform a short skit to educate people about the cause, symptoms, and treatment of the disease.

Mammals have lungs that expand to allow oxygen to enter the body. When mammals exhale, the lungs relax and release carbon dioxide into the atmosphere.

Some living creatures take in oxygen without the use of lungs. Research a creature such as a fish, an earthworm, or an octopus, and write an explanation of its respiratory process.

The iron lung is a machine that was used in the 1940s and 1950s to help people survive a disease called polio. This machine helped people who were unable to breathe by moving the chest muscles so air could enter the lungs.

Since 1950 there have been many improvements in the medical world. Give an oral presentation explaining one medical breakthrough that occurred after 1950.

Air leaving the lungs is used to make the vocal cords vibrate and produce the sound necessary for speech.

Experiment with sound, exhalation, and lung capacity. Ask friends to take one deep breath and then exhale while singing a note. Count seconds from the time the note begins until it ends to measure each person's lung capacity. Make a graph to show your results.

Though the lungs fill with air automatically as you breathe, the process takes 3% of your body's energy.

If breathing takes 3% of the body's energy, other activities can account for the other 97%. Brainstorm a list of body functions and muscular activities. Analyze the list and predict how much of the body's energy is used for each activity. Compare your list with those of your classmates.

Community Action Project

The Bronchi

The bronchi are two large tubes leading to the lungs. These tubes carry air to the lungs to give the body the oxygen it needs to live.

- The bronchi are shaped like two upside-down trees leading to each lung.
- The bronchi lead to small tubes called secondary and tertiary bronchi inside each lung. The secondary and tertiary bronchi branch off into smaller tubes called bronchioles. The bronchioles lead to air sacs called alveoli.
- Mucus, a sticky fluid, lines the bronchi to trap foreign substances that could harm the lungs. Mucus is pushed up to the throat for removal by cilia, tiny hair-like structures, that also line the bronchi. At times, mucus cannot trap all of the foreign substances that are inhaled.

INFORMATION

Lung cancer is a disease that usually affects adult men and women. Most cases of lung cancer begin in the cells of the bronchi. Bronchial cells that are otherwise healthy can multiply too quickly, clump together, and turn into cancer cells. The cancer cells form a mass called a tumor. The tumor blocks the bronchi so air cannot enter the lung easily and does not allow the mucus to escape the lung. Surgeons must remove the tumor completely or the cancer cells will spread throughout the body and eventually cause death. About 85% of all lung cancer cases are associated with cigarette smoking. The best way to deter lung cancer is to not smoke.

Helping Others—Anti-Smoking Education

Research

Research cigarette smoking and lung cancer. Contact the American Lung Association for information. Design and perform a half-hour-long presentation for kindergarten through third-grade students to teach the dangers of cigarette smoking.

Action Plan

Use these questions to help make your plan.

- What adult can help organize your presentation? Which friends might like to present with you?
- Which class might like to hear your presentation? How can you contact a primary-grade teacher to set up a time, date, and location for your program?
- What facts about smoking are most important to share with young children? How can you share these facts in an entertaining manner?
- Some parents smoke cigarettes. How can you get your message across without sounding disrespectful or judgmental?
- Young children remember information when it is presented in an easy song or poem. Can you write a catchy tune or poem to teach kids that smoking is harmful?
- What could you make to give students as a reminder not to smoke?
- Are there any special props or materials needed for your presentation? Make a list of what you need.
- It is important to rehearse a presentation many times. When and where can you rehearse?

Anatomy © 2003 Creative Teaching Press

Focus on Allergies and the Respiratory System

Are you sniffly around cats? Does every spring bring warm weather for everyone else but a runny nose for you? You might have allergies to certain substances. Some of the most common types of allergies are to pollen of trees and grasses, spores of molds, dust mites, and animal dander. Reactions range from mild itchiness in your throat, nose, and eyes, to a severe and life-threatening asthma attack.

How Does It Happen?

The allergen—for example, pollen—enters the respiratory system through the nose. It irritates the cilia, which are tiny hairs that line the nose. They lengthen in response to the irritation. Your nose might feel itchy. You might start sneezing.

Then the allergen causes chemical reactions that tell the body to start producing extra mucus. The body is trying to wash away the allergen by trapping it in the mucus and sweeping it up and out of the lungs. To you, this will feel like a runny nose and a sore throat.

If you are especially sensitive to an allergen, the body might start chemical reactions that cause the muscles in your lungs to tighten up. Combined with all that extra mucus, it suddenly feels like you have a very large weight on your chest. You just cannot get a good, deep breath. You make wheezing sounds as you breathe, and you feel tired.

Luckily, there are lots of medicines available to allergy sufferers. Some prevent an attack from happening when you take them on a regular basis. Other medicines treat the symptoms after the attack has already begun. Either way, they can make you feel a lot better!

normal airway   narrowed airway

Write About It

Have you ever had an allergic reaction to something? Write about the experience in a narrative paragraph. Or, conduct research to gather more information on allergies, and write an informative essay on the topic. Share your finished work with the class.

Did You Know?

Allergies can also cause reactions that are not related to your respiratory system. Some rashes may be a symptom of an allergic reaction to foods you are eating or chemicals in your environment.

What Did You Learn?

A. Circle the best answer.

1. Which is not a part of the respiratory system?

a. bronchi
b. clavicle
c. trachea
d. alveoli

2. As you inhale, oxygen from the air

a. turns into food through a process called photosynthesis.
b. helps inflate a balloon.
c. is exchanged for CO_2 when given to the tissue cells.
d. fills up a milk jug.

B. Draw a line to complete each sentence.

1. The trachea
2. The alveoli
3. The bronchi

a. is also called the windpipe.
b. branch into the right and left lungs.
c. are small chambers that work like tiny balloons that inflate with inhalation and deflate with exhalation.

C. Fill in each blank. Use *diaphram, allergens, pollen,* **and** *oxygen.*

1. When your body tries to wash away _____ in the bronchi, you develop a runny nose.
2. Inhalation occurs when the _____ tightens up, or contracts.
3. During exercise the body requires additional _____.
4. _____ is a very common allergen.

D. Explain how the diaphragm causes you to inhale and exhale.

_____

_____

_____

_____

Anatomy © 2003 Creative Teaching Press

Name _____

The Digestive System

The Digestive System and Alimentary Canal

The digestive system converts food into energy. This complex system breaks down carbohydrates, proteins, and fats from foods into molecules small enough for the body to use.

The alimentary canal is the main part of the digestive system. This canal is a series of organs which starts at the mouth and ends at the rectum.

FOOD'S JOURNEY

Use the diagram of the alimentary canal to obtain the information needed to complete the sentences. The sentences are in order.

1. Food first enters the _____.
   _____ _____ under the tongue secrete digestive juices.

2. Food leaves the mouth and enters the _____, an opening between the mouth and nasal cavities.

3. Food is squeezed down by muscles through the _____, a tube that runs from the pharynx to the stomach.

4. Food then enters an elastic muscular bag called the _____. This bag churns and squeezes the food while mixing it with digestive juices.

5. After food leaves the stomach, it enters a 20-foot-long, thin tube called the _____ _____ where the food's nutrients are eventually absorbed into the bloodstream.

6. Food that has not been used in the small intestine moves on to a thick tube, about 5 feet long, called the _____ _____. This tube converts the food into feces—a combination of undigested food, water, and bacteria.

7. Feces, food converted to semi-solid waste, leaves the large intestine and it is held in a short tube called the _____ until it is expelled from the body.

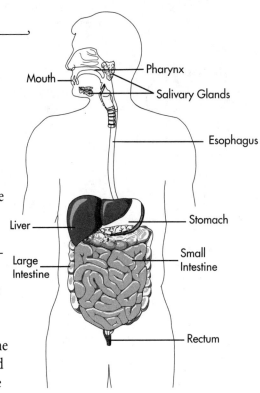

Mouth — Pharynx

Salivary Glands

Esophagus

Liver — Stomach

Large Intestine — Small Intestine

Rectum

Testing for Carbohydrates, Protein, and Fat

The digestive system breaks down the carbohydrates, proteins, and fats from food. The digestive system also distributes these nutrients into the bloodstream to give the body energy and to help it grow.

Carbohydrates are found in sugary or starchy foods. Carbohydrates break down into simple sugars called glucose and glycogen. Glucose provides instant energy for the body. Glycogen provides storable energy.

Proteins are found in both vegetables and meat and are essential to build and repair body cells.

Fat, also essential for the body, is found in dairy products, oily foods, and meat. Fat provides storable energy and acts as insulation to help control body temperature. Since storing excess fat is dangerous for the body's health, it is important to limit the amount of fat eaten.

FOOD TESTS

Foods can be tested for the presence of carbohydrates, proteins, and fats. Gather five or six foods and complete the following tests.

1. Gather iodine, biuret reagent, a brown paper towel, two eyedroppers, and three paper plates. Set aside.
2. Gather five or six foods such as pieces of potato, banana, macaroni, or bread. Divide the food samples into thirds and place each set on a paper plate.
3. Using the foods you chose, make a chart similar to the one shown.
4. To test for the presence of carbohydrates, use one set of food samples. Place two or three drops of iodine on each food in the set. If the iodine drops turn from brownish orange to purple-black, the food contains carbohydrates. Place a check on the chart next to the foods where carbohydrates are present.

5. To test for proteins, use another set of food samples. Use a clean eyedropper and place two or three drops of biuret reagent on each food. If the biuret reagent turns from blue to purple, protein is present in the food. Mark your chart to indicate foods with protein.
6. To test for fats, place a set of foods on a brown paper towel. Set aside. After 15 minutes, remove the food from the paper towel. Touch the paper towel. Does it feel wet or does it feel greasy? Hold the paper towel up to the light. Can you see light through it? If the paper towel feels greasy and you can see light through it, fat is present. Mark your graph.
7. Analyze your results. Which foods contain all three essential ingredients? Which foods seem to be high in fat content? Which foods seem to be low in fat? Which foods seem to be best for your body?

Anatomy © 2003 Creative Teaching Press

Liver and Gall Bladder Task Cards

NOTE TO TEACHER: There are dozens of ways to use these task cards. Here are just a few…

- Laminate cards, cut them out, and place them in a learning center.
- Send a task card with each student during library research time.
- Assign cards as a long-term homework project or as extra credit.
- Pass cards out randomly, one to each student. Have students form groups according to card tasks to complete the tasks together.

Your liver is like a factory. The liver has a production department that makes and stores a digestive fluid called bile. It has a warehouse that stores digested food from the blood. Your liver also has a recycling department that filters poisons and wastes from the blood.

Research how your liver works. Draw a diagram of an imaginary liver "factory." Label and describe the liver's departments and functions.

Your liver manufactures bile, a yellowish-green fluid, and stores it in the gall bladder. Bile acts like a grease-fighting detergent, breaking up globs of fat into small particles to prepare the fat for digestion.

Show the action of bile by putting equal amounts of oil and water in a glass. Shake it and note the results. Now add grease-fighting detergent or stain remover. Shake it again. How does bile act like the detergent?

A gland is any body organ which secretes a substance that changes blood so the body can use it. Your liver is the largest gland in the body, weighing between three and four pounds.

Research body systems to make a list of five glands. Include the liver. Write the name of each gland and its function.

Bile and cholesterol can stagnate in your gall bladder and form small lumps called gallstones. Gallstones are rock hard and have sharp edges that are very painful. Gallstones either pass through your digestive system naturally or must be removed through surgery.

Use research to develop 10 questions about what it is like to experience gallstones. Use the questions to interview a medical doctor.

Your gall bladder is a pear-shaped sac that holds and releases bile produced by the liver. The gall bladder and liver work together to aid in digestion.

Study the interaction between your liver and gall bladder. Imagine you are the liver. Write a thank-you letter to the gall bladder telling the reasons why you appreciate it.

Hepatitis is a disease that causes an inflammation of the liver. There are three types of hepatitis: Hepatitis A, Hepatitis B, and Non-A Non-B Hepatitis.

Research hepatitis. Make a Venn diagram that compares two of the three kinds of hepatitis.

Your liver filters poisons, such as alcohol and drugs, from the bloodstream. Your liver can lose its ability to function over a period of time if too much poison has been filtered.

Use research to create a commercial about the physical dangers of alcohol and drug use. Perform or videotape your commercial.

Your liver has the ability to renew and repair itself. A whole lobe of the liver that has been removed can miraculously replace itself within four weeks.

Make two comparative lists; one listing body parts and functions that can renew or replace themselves and one listing those that cannot.

Community Action Project

The Stomach

The stomach is a large bag-like part of the alimentary canal that breaks down food into a creamy paste called chyme. The stomach stores the chyme until it is ready to move into the small intestine.

- The stomach is a j-shaped muscular bag leading from the esophagus to the small intestine.
- During digestion, the enzyme *pepsin* is secreted by the stomach to aid in the digestion of milk and protein. The stomach also secretes a substance called the intrinsic factor that allows the body to absorb vitamin B12.
- One important function of the stomach is to secrete a digestive juice called hydrochloric acid. Hydrochloric acid kills harmful bacteria in food.

INFORMATION

Stress is a body condition that occurs when a person is feeling nervous, frightened, angry, or anxious. When a person is feeling stress, he or she may develop many physical symptoms. One symptom of prolonged stress is the formation of open sores in the stomach called stomach ulcers.

Another name for stomach ulcers is gastric ulcers. Gastric ulcers occur when digestive juices eat through a weakened stomach lining creating an open wound.

One way to reduce the risk of gastric ulcers is to reduce stress. Three ways to eliminate stress from your life are to exercise regularly, eat healthy foods, and practice relaxation techniques.

Helping Others—Managing Stress/A Health Fair

Research

Research stress management through one aspect: exercise, proper nutrition, or relaxation techniques. Use your knowledge to plan a health fair booth that provides information and demonstrations to educate people about the affects of stress and stress management.

Action Plan

Use these questions to help make your plan.

- What stress management information is most important to share with people?
- How can you present your research in an interesting and entertaining way? Demonstrations? Giveaways?
- You may be able to convince a health care professional to help in your booth. Whom could you contact? What service could this person provide?
- How will you make and decorate your booth?
- Who in your community might like to attend a health fair? How can you advertise the health fair and your booth?
- How might you make your booth interactive?

Anatomy © 2003 Creative Teaching Press

Focus on Taste

Think about all the different foods you eat over the course of a year. Would you be surprised to know that they are all made up of only four basic tastes? Your tongue senses four tastes: bitter, sour, salty, and sweet. It is the combination of these tastes that gives each food its own flavor.

Your tongue is made up of lots of little bumps. Only some of these bumps are used for tasting. The bumps have taste buds on their sides—not on top as you might think. When you eat, the food dissolves in your saliva, and the saliva sinks into your tongue and comes in contact with the taste buds. It all happens very quickly.

Each taste bud is sensitive to one particular kind of taste. Taste buds that are sensitive to the same taste are grouped together on the tongue. We taste sweet and salty with the front of our tongue. We taste bitter and sour with the back.

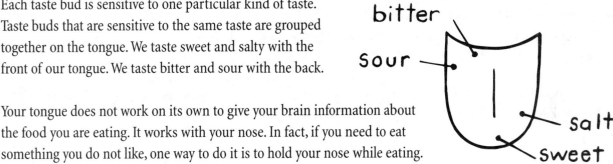

Your tongue does not work on its own to give your brain information about the food you are eating. It works with your nose. In fact, if you need to eat something you do not like, one way to do it is to hold your nose while eating. It will dramatically reduce your ability to "taste." In fact, your sense of smell is 20,000 times stronger than your sense of taste. Your nose can detect about 10,000 different smells. Smell does not just help you enjoy the food you eat; it also helps you want to eat in the first place. This is a part of the reason why you may not be as hungry when you have a stuffed-up nose. Smell receptors deep inside your nose help trigger feelings of hunger, and they cannot do that when they are covered in mucus.

Try It!
Materials
- blindfold
- several different-flavored jelly beans (2 of each flavor)
- cup of water

Find a partner to help you explore this activity on taste. Blindfold your partner, and have your partner firmly hold his or her nose. Sort the jelly beans into two groups, with one jelly bean of each flavor in each group. Give your partner a sip of water and a jelly bean to taste. Ask your partner to identify the flavor, and record the response. Continue with the remaining jelly beans. Then, repeat the experiment with the second group of jelly beans, but this time, do not have your partner close his or her nose. Does your partner's accuracy improve?

Did You Know?
Your tongue does not just sense taste—it also senses texture and temperature. We use this information to determine food safety as well as to decide if we like food or not. Room temperature potato salad should make us stop and think. Your tongue also has a rough surface that helps you keep food in your mouth and move it around for tasting, chewing, and swallowing.

What Did You Learn?

A. Circle the best answer.

1. How many different smells can your nose distinguish?

a. 4
b. 100
c. 400
d. 10,000

2. Which organ can renew and repair itself?

a. the esophagus
b. the liver
c. the lungs
d. the pancreas

B. Draw a line to complete each sentence.

1. The esophagus
2. The gall bladder
3. The liver
4. The large intestine
5. The pancreas

a. produces digestive juices to break down food.
b. absorbs water from the remaining food.
c. is a pear-shaped sac that stores bile until it is needed.
d. squeezes food down to the stomach by muscle movements.
e. cleans the blood by filtering poisons and wastes.

C. Fill in each blank.

1. Smell receptors in your nose help trigger feelings of _____.
2. Your tongue can taste salty, sweet, bitter, and _____.

D. Describe the path a bite of food takes through your digestive system.

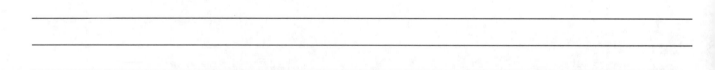